The Ultimate Gentleman

The Handbook 2.0

Mr. Lynn Johnson

To my little gentlemen Jacob and Luke,

Always share the Spirit of Love in all that you say and do!

Love,

Dad

Definition of a Gentleman

"A gentleman is one who never hurts anyone's feelings unintentionally."

- Oscar Wilde

"Anyone can be heroic from time to time, but a gentleman is something you have to be all the time."

- Luigi Pirandello

"A gentleman is one who puts more into the world than he takes out."

- George Bernard Shaw

"Courtesy is as much a mark of a gentleman as courage."

- Theodore Roosevelt

"When you wear a bow tie, doors open for you. Your posture is a little more erect; your shoulders are a little further back; your style is a little more dynamic. It's about the reestablishment of the gentleman."

- Dhani Jones

"A gentleman has his eyes on all those present; he is tender toward the bashful, gentle toward the distant, and merciful toward the absent."

- Lawrence G. Lovasik

"This is the final test of a gentleman: his respect for those who can be of no possible service to him."

- William Lyon Phelps

"A gentleman is simply a patient wolf."

- Lana Turner

"The true gentleman is a man whose conduct proceeds from good will and an acute sense of propriety, and whose self-control is equal to all emergencies;

Who does not make the poor man conscious of his poverty, the obscure man of his obscurity, or any man of his inferiority or deformity;

Who is himself humbled if necessity compels him to humble another;

Who does not flatter wealth, cringe before power, or boast of his own possessions or achievements;

Who speaks with frankness but always with sincerity and sympathy;

Whose deed follows his word;

Who thinks of the rights and feelings of others, rather than his own; and who appears well in any company, a man with whom honor is sacred and virtue safe."

- John Walter Wayland

Table of Contents

Forward

In the mid-1940s, Coach Charles "Chappie" Davis founded a sports club for African American boys in his local community, dubbing them "The Sophisticated Gents." These young men grow up to become successful athletes and looked up to as heroes in their community. As the years pass they form a bond that would last a lifetime. After twenty-five years the members of the Gents decide to hold a testimonial dinner for Coach Chappie to recognize him for the impact he had on their lives.

This is the plot summary to a 1981 television mini-series called "The Sophisticated Gents." The last time I saw this movie I was 10 years old. Even though more than thirty years have passed, this movie left a long lasting impression in my mind. Although I can barely remember the storyline, it was the first time I ever saw men that I thought of as gentlemen.

Whenever I watch a movie that rewinds back to the days of well-mannered, well-dressed and highly charismatic men, it becomes clear that in present culture, there are fewer and fewer gentlemen to be found. There was a time when clothes were sharper, immaturity shorter and being a gentleman meant something. Now it seems as if there is something missing, something stripped from men today besides fedora's and blazers.

Although appearance isn't everything, in today's reality we make decisions about people within the first three seconds of meeting them. We then spend the next ninety seconds trying to confirm our first impressions. This means that before we even open our mouth we've been sized up and profiled. Knowing this, we should always dress neatly, professionally, and appropriately. The fact is you never know who you are going to meet, so like it or not, someone will form their initial impression of you based on how you look. You shouldn't judge a book by its cover, but in our fast paced society a book's cover can be just as important as its content. In a competitive and outwardly judgmental world it pays to understand the importance of your clothing and grooming. Investing the proper resources into your personal presentation will multiply your ability to succeed.

The Ultimate Gentleman: The Handbook 2.0 provides essential information for men on how to have a clean, elegant and sophisticated appearance. In essence, bring back the lost art of being a gentleman. This handbook also shares qualities that make a good man. The *"ultimate gentleman"* is defined as a man who not only has a refined appearance and charismatic personality, but a man who is well-mannered and educated with high standards of proper behavior. The *ultimate gentleman* performs at the highest level in his role as a provider, leader, teacher, and relationship builder. These roles require a man to possess high character – treating others with respect and courtesy. It also means he should represent masculinity and manliness.

My hope is that this handbook will not only influence men to be their best, but serve as a guide for those who have limited opportunities to view and learn from them. This small handbook can also be a valuable resource to help boys and young men from all backgrounds to become adult men who are positive and influential in relationships, family, church and community. I sincerely hope you or someone you know will find *The Ultimate Gentleman: The Handbook 2.0* a useful tool for personal growth and success.

God bless you and thank you for your support!

Mr. Lynn Johnson
Founder & Proprietor of UltimateGents.com
President & Senior Partner of
Johnson Development Group, LLC

The Ultimate Gentleman's Top 75 Tips

The following tips have been compiled for men who want to take on the character and status of being the "ultimate gentleman". Although everyone may not agree with all the tips shared, most of them are meant to be subjective and not intended to offend anyone.

Simply put, these tips and suggestions help men to bring back the lost art of being a gentleman.

CHARACTER

№75 **A gentleman is well-mannered and courteous.** The ultimate gentleman is polite to everyone in action and words.

№74 **A gentleman should never use profanity.** A man uses profanity because he doesn't have the words to say what's on his mind. Furthermore, it is always very effortless and indecorous to use expletives.

№73 **A gentleman is always in control of his mind and body.** Refrain from passing gas, burping, or talking too loud in public. If you have to pass gas, excuse yourself to the men's room.

№72 **A gentleman always sits up straight!** Never slouch your shoulders! Keep your head up when you walk. The ultimate gentleman maintains excellent posture.

№71 **A gentleman should seldom fight!** However, he never acts like a coward. If challenged, stand up for yourself and what you believe. Don't sacrifice your values for some bum who woke up on the wrong side of the bed. If someone is simply running their mouth, don't embarrass yourself, just walk away! The ultimate gentleman knows that fighting is one of the worst ways to solve problems. Be wise; don't get punched, shot or stabbed trying to be a hero. Know the difference between standing up for yourself and being a fool.

№**70** **A gentleman does all he can to be honest and upfront.** Always say what you mean and mean what you say. If you promise something, stick to it. The ultimate gentleman keeps his word.

№**69** **A gentleman is always in control.** Don't drink alcohol excessively. It can impair your judgment and a true gentleman is in control of himself at all times. The ultimate gentleman keeps a natural high.

№**68** **A gentleman is humble and thoughtful.** Never think or act like you are better than anyone else. Avoid seeming pompous; be modest instead of showing off what you know.

№**67** **A gentleman is always on top of his game.** Never wait for something bad to happen to be proactive. Always have a plan. The ultimate gentleman makes things happen and is prepared for whatever happens.

№**66** **A gentleman understands that the world is bigger than the block he grew up on.** Being open-minded and aware of the world around you shows class and sophistication. Travel to a place you can't pronounce. If you can't travel...read! The ultimate gentleman makes the world his classroom.

№**65** **A gentleman stays informed.** Watch the news or listen to the radio, preferably more than one channel. Get different perspectives whether you agree with them or not. Also, read the newspaper or magazines. However, try not to go straight to the sports section of the newspaper.

Read the business or even the neighborhood sections first.

№64 **A gentleman is confident with his political and religious views.** If you are asked about your opinions don't be afraid to give them. Don't steer clear of discussing political and religious topics simply to circumvent hurting someone's feelings. The ultimate gentleman uses discretion and intelligence to communicate his feelings and opinions to others who may disagree or feel offended. Hold off on fighting the power until you get to know someone.

№63 **A gentleman knows the difference between friends, colleagues and co-workers.** Friends are the people you go through things with; colleagues are the people you do business with; and co-workers are the people you get forced into a relationship with. Relationship boundaries can be very gray; however, the ultimate gentleman keeps all his relationships in perspective.

№62 **A gentleman never flaunts what he has.** No matter how valuable or cutting-edge your possessions may be, never talk-up or flash them in the face of others. Nothing is wrong with using your resources to obtain the latest technology, however no one likes a show-off. The ultimate gentleman conceals his gadgets like 007 Agent James Bond. You won't know his Rolex watch is a bomb until he has no choice but to use it.

№61 **A gentleman is polite to everyone.** Always be aware of how you can help people. Wait an extra few seconds to hold the door for the person behind you. Offer to help an elderly or pregnant lady get their grocery bags to the car. Even if you don't like someone, be polite and courteous; show that you're the better man.

№60 **A gentleman keeps his temper under control.** Nobody's perfect, but when you lose your temper, you're showing everyone that you can't control your emotions. If you can't control your emotions, then how can you possibly control anything else? The ultimate gentleman can keep his cool at all times.

№59 **A gentleman never yells.** When you yell, it raises the stress level of the people around you. It implies that you can't reason with people and rely on intimidation to get your point across. Yelling or even talking too loudly makes people think you need attention. Don't be that guy! The ultimate gentleman doesn't have to yell to get attention. He simply commands it with his presence.

№58 **A gentleman never speaks negatively about others.** Never say something about a person to someone else unless you have already shared it with the person you are talking about. People say negative things about others to make themselves feel good. The ultimate gentleman strives to be positive in all that he says and does. Like the old saying goes, if you can't say something good (about someone), then don't say anything.

PROFESSIONAL DEMEANOR

№57 **A gentleman understands how to carry himself in a meeting.** Be on time to meetings – early if you can. Look people in the eyes when you greet them and give a firm handshake. Don't hold conversations at the same time someone else is talking. The ultimate gentleman lets others finish their point before giving his.

№56 **A gentleman never laughs at the mistakes of others.** In short of being cruel, this is downright childish. When you mess up, the last thing you want is for someone not only to bring it to your attention, but to ridicule you on top of it. The ultimate gentleman is a man not a child!

№55 **A gentleman understands how to give and receive constructive criticism.** You can improve personally and professionally by being open to constructive criticism. When you receive criticism, don't get too defensive. Take what is shared and fix it. Even if the person sharing doesn't have your best interest in mind, be the bigger person. This could be your time to shine. When you give criticism, focus on the facts. Don't offer solutions, yet make yourself available to them if they need help.

№54 **A gentleman earns the respect of his co-workers and subordinates.** Never expect it nor try and demand it. Never talk down to someone simply because of what you do, where you are from or who you know. Keep in mind that the person you talk down to could end up being your boss. The ultimate gentleman knows that the people he abuses on the way up could be the same people he passes on his way down!

№53 **A gentleman never does anything simply to make money.** Learn the difference between a good investment and a bad investment. Sure you will make mistakes. In fact, if you haven't made any mistakes, then you may not be moving forward. The ultimate gentleman never compromises his integrity to make money. Take farmers for example, they have to know the difference between good and bad soil. If they know that the soil is bad, they plant where they know a harvest will grow.

№52 **A gentleman is careful about what he says in letters, e-mails and texts.** Electronic and paper correspondence is permanent and can be used for or against you. The ultimate gentleman meticulously reviews his messages, editing if necessary to make sure recipients will understand what he's saying — and in the tone in which he wants to convey.

№51 **A gentleman knows when to ask for help.** Surround yourself with people who will make your job easier. You can't do everything by yourself, so don't try. Positive relationships with people can be pivotal to your success. Always thank them and show your appreciation when they come through for you. The ultimate gentleman never tries to be the smartest person in the room, but also not the dumbest. You should always seek to learn from others while still being in a position to teach others what you know.

№50 **A gentleman never responds to a text or answers his cell phone while in the middle of a face-to-face conversation.** The same rule applies if you are in a meeting, at church or at dinner, unless it is an emergency. Do not attempt to drive or walk and send text messages simultaneously.

№49 **A gentleman uses his imagination as well as his intellect.** Even if you can boast about a high IQ never lose sight of the power of the imagination. The greatest inventions or discoveries have been achieved through the existence of a profound imaginative intelligence. The ultimate gentleman always dreams and imagines the possibilities.

№48 **A gentleman makes every day a masterpiece.**

№47 **A gentleman minds his own business.** Just because you work 40 hours a week at someone else's business doesn't mean you should forget about your own. I'm sure that the people you work for have a plan for retirement, but do you? The ultimate gentleman manages his business affairs as diligent as he would for the people he works for. It makes no sense to generate millions for someone else and you only produce hundreds for yourself!

№46 **A gentleman is always prepared to perform three jobs.** His own, his employees, and his boss. The ultimate gentleman plans for all possibilities at work. You never know when you could be promoted or demoted.

№45 **A gentleman knows the difference between saving and investing.** You save by keeping something for yourself, to be used for its value at a later date. You invest by giving something away, with hopes of getting it returned with increased value by a later date. The ultimate gentleman does both.

PUBLIC & DINING ETIQUETTE

№44 **A gentleman knows how to dine with a lady.** Open her door. Pull out her chair. Let her order first. Wait until a she receives her food before you begin to eat.

№43 **A gentleman knows how to dine with a group.** Take a seat before you start eating. Wait until everyone in your party has arrived and is seated before you begin eating. A subtle rule is that everyone should start dining at the same time. If you initiate a dinner date or meeting, then you should expect to pay.

№42 **A gentleman uses proper dining etiquette.** Know the difference between a dinner and salad fork. When finished eating, always place your knife and fork on your plate side by side in a 45-degree angle. Place your napkin in your lap before you eat. Stuffing it in your shirt is grounds for getting slapped. The ultimate gentleman avoids chewing or talking with his mouth open.

№41 **A gentleman learns about restaurants and where to eat economically.** Use the internet, local guides, or word of mouth to find a variety of restaurants that appeal to different taste buds. When dining out, the ultimate gentleman always tips no less than 20 percent. Tips are often times a server's livelihood. Don't let someone else cover the tip if you invited them out.

№ 40   **A gentleman doesn't spit in the presence of a lady.** Many men do this almost subconsciously. Spitting is very crude and not attractive for a lady to look at. The ultimate gentleman doesn't spend five minutes clearing his throat only to shoot a glob across the way. This is an unacceptable practice! Go to the restroom.

№ 39   **A gentleman should always remove his hat indoors.** This concept seems to have gone out the window these days; however, a man should remove headwear upon entering a building. The ultimate gentleman is also prepared to remove his shoes if requested to do so at someone's home. Remember to always wear clean socks!

№ 38   **A gentleman always gives another gentleman his space.** If you walk into a public men's room and there are seven empty stalls except one, don't walk up and use the stall right next to the only guy taking a leak. Give a man some room. The personal space barrier has been breached! The ultimate gentleman always washes his hands after using the restroom! One in four men don't wash their hands after a trip to the restroom.

№ 37   **A gentleman does what most men don't do (anymore).** When a lady enters a room stand. Be prepared to take off her coat or pull out her chair. This standard of etiquette has been somewhat relaxed, so you can stand upon entrance but remain seated upon exit. This is a simple but powerful action. If you are single, this is a great way to make a first impression with a lady you might want to get to know. If you are married, then nothing short of this standard is accepted. The ultimate gentleman

understands that proper etiquette may put you a head
and shoulder above the other men in the room.

GROOMING & HYGIENE

№36 **A gentleman makes a great first impression.** First
impressions are important and your face is where people
make their initial assumptions about what kind of a
person you are. It is important to keep your face clean. A
mild soap can take care of this. There are facial scrubs
that deep clean your pores and removes the dead skin
that leaves your face dull. The ultimate gentleman should
shine even on a cloudy day!

№35 **A gentleman keeps himself fresh and clean.** Maintaining
excellent hygiene is a must. Don't just use a bar of soap,
lather up a wash cloth and scrub yourself. Make sure your
ears have no wax in them and that privates and facial hair
are clean. When applying deodorant or cologne, don't use
too much. You want to have a pleasing scent, one to be
remembered by, not one that can clear a room.

№34 **A gentleman keeps his breath fresh.** Brush your teeth,
gargle or have a breath mint before getting up close and
personal. Paying attention to your breath will ensure that
others don't have to.

№33 **A gentleman goes the extra mile in making sure his
hygiene is proper.** Keep your hands and nails clean and
your mustache and beard trimmed to achieve an overall
healthy look. The ultimate gentleman will make sure his
toe and foot game are up to par. Unkept hands and feet
are not only unattractive, but can be unhealthy too.
Manicures and pedicures are available for men. Your
fingers and toes are important. Your hands and feet have
a big job in life and need some TLC!

№32 **A gentleman always carries a comb or brush to keep his hair neat.** If you have a messier style, keep it out of your eyes. Get regular haircuts. Ultimate gentlemen don't wear bangs.

CLOTHING, CLASS & STYLE

№31 **A gentleman looks his best at all times.** Wear clothes that fit your body type and eliminate flashy clothing. Avoid trends that make you look like everybody else. Some fashion items should be banned all together such as banana yellow suits, fire engine red sport coats, or a wrist watch as big as a wall clock. The ultimate gentleman's wardrobe should be current, but not so trendy that he loses his individual style.

№30 **A gentleman can look good in whatever he wears.** Looking good doesn't mean you can't wear jeans, t-shirts, and sneakers. It just means that they should be clean and unwrinkled. At the end of the day, the ultimate gentleman knows it's the guy inside the clothes that counts.

№29 **A gentleman owns at least one tailored suit or at least a well-made off-the-rack suit.** Find a good tailor. Know your measurements and sizes. Have at least one pair of black lace-up shoes. If you buy one pair of shoes and one suit per year, you'll have a nice wardrobe collection. The ultimate gentleman invests in his wardrobe.

№28 **A gentleman knows how to do his own laundry.** If you can't make it to the cleaners, learn how to launder you own shirts. A hot iron and a can of spray starch can do wonders.

№27   **Top 10 Faux Pas of Style**

  1. Never wear a belt with suspenders.

  2. Never wear the same pair of pants two days in a row.

  3. Never layer collared shirts.

  4. Never wear brown shoes with a black suit.

  5. Never match your socks with your shirt.

  6. Never button the top button of a polo shirt.

  7. Never tuck your sweater into your trousers.

  8. Never wear socks with sandals or flip flops. Simply terrible!

  9. Never wear a clip-on tie.

  10. Never try to out dress your lady. Being a gentleman isn't "metro".

№26   **A gentleman never alters or adds to his appearance to make him look better.** Color contact lenses, hair extensions, make-up, or surgical procedures are unacceptable. The ultimate gentleman is confident with who he is and accepts what he looks likes. The only exception to this tip would be for medical or health reasons. You also don't want to be vain. A good looking man should also be a good man.

№25   **A gentleman is culturally diverse.** Take time to learn more about people in ways other than watching television. Attend cultural events, visit museums or your local city market. The ultimate gentleman is cultured enough so that he can order from a menu written in French or can give the proper greeting to someone if he travels to China.

№**24** **A gentleman can cook.** Even if cooking is not your thing, learn to at least prepare breakfast. Your lady will love to wake up to the smell of a fresh omelet.

№**23** **A gentleman knows the difference between wearing baggy jeans and saggy jeans.** You can wear pants that are loose or even slightly baggy, but never wear saggy pants. Showing your butt and underwear is not appealing in any setting. Wear a belt. However, the ultimate gentleman never wears pants that are too tight. Fitted jeans are cool as long as you don't wander in to nut-buddy land. No gentleman should ever be seen in skinny jeans. Men over 40, let it go!

RELATIONSHIPS

№**22** **A gentleman becomes one with his spouse.** However, never abandon your mother regardless if your relationship with her is good, bad or indifferent. Any man who dishonors his mother or father should not be surprised if his children dishonor him!

№**21** **A gentleman never stares at a lady he doesn't know, unless he plans to get to know her.** If you do stare, move in quickly. Prolonged staring is equivalent to stalking. You don't want to intimidate or scare a lady.

№**20** **A gentleman lets a woman know if he wants to be in a serious relationship.** If you don't, let her know. Don't play games! If you do, tell her, but don't be too aggressive too fast. Don't use the "L" word just after the first date. The ultimate gentleman is open and honest about sharing his feelings. Express yourself to her and expect the same in return. If the feelings are not mutual, pump your brakes...you might just be in the "just friends" zone!

№**19** **A gentleman wants to look his best for his lady.** Never get to close to a lady if you haven't had a bath. Apart from giving personal space, attempting to get too close to her when you stink will get you rejected every time. If she's cool with your funk, stop reading this book and hand it to someone who can make good use of it.

№18 **A gentleman never asks a lady out and expects her to pay.** A Dutch evening is never acceptable.

№17 **A gentleman is never embarrassed by his lady.** Always introduce her to your friends, colleagues or co-workers. The ultimate gentleman never introduces the special lady in his life as his girlfriend. She is either your wife or your friend. A girlfriend is something you have in high school!

№16 **A gentleman behaves as though chivalry isn't dead!** When you're with your special lady remember to always do nice things for her. Carry her bags, pump her gas, open her door, and always ask if she needs anything. Do spontaneous things like delivering her flowers with a card, leave a rose and a love note on her pillow, or make her breakfast in bed. Don't concern yourself with how expensive or flashy these kind acts may be, it's about the effort that you put into making your lady feel like a queen. However, the ultimate gentleman understands while being chivalrous is nice, don't be overbearing.

№15 **A gentleman must always be ready to plan something special.** Lead the way when it comes to planning activities and events with your lady. It doesn't have to be expensive or complicated. Simple and pleasant works just fine. Take charge every once in a while and suggest she wears something that you like. The ultimate gentleman is somewhat of a renaissance man. Don't just take her to dinner and a movie, have lunch in the park. Prepare a picnic basket with some simple sandwiches, fruit and a special bottle of wine. Afterwards go salsa dancing!

№ 14   **A gentleman avoids arguing with his lady in public.** Keep things private to let her know there's an exclusive world that you and her share. Be in control of your emotions and actions. Whether she is your friend or spouse, a lady wants to know that even in the midst of a difficult situation that you will maintain your composure.

№ 13   **A gentleman stands up for his lady.** However, everyone who looks at her isn't trying to jump her bones! When someone starts giving her strange looks or unwanted advances, intervene. Wrap your arm around her waist or shoulder and walk away. The physical contact reassures her and lets the antagonist know he has to deal with you if he approaches.

№ 12   **A gentleman accepts the fact that he is a gentleman.** If a lady doesn't respect you for who you are, she isn't worth it. If you've made yourself a worthy catch, the person you are with should treat you like it. If she doesn't, you might be setting yourself up for heartache. The ultimate gentleman knows the difference between being wise and being a fool!

№ 11   **A gentleman never talks about himself too much!** Remember to hold a little bit back but share just enough to peak interest about who you are. Overindulging a lady about what you do for a living can be a big turn-off. When you meet a lady for the first time you want to ask general questions and expect the same in return. Never dig too deep into her personal life until you have at least been on several dates. The ultimate gentleman keeps his conversation positive and upbeat. He always shares just enough about himself to keep her coming back for more!

THE ULTIMATE TOP TEN

№10 The ultimate gentleman **models the behaviors of good men**.

№9 The ultimate gentleman **has an appreciation for education**.

№8 The ultimate gentleman **keeps a healthy network of relationships**.

№7 The ultimate gentleman **maintains excellent mental and physical health**.

№6 The ultimate gentleman **nurtures his personal talents, skills and abilities**.

№5 The ultimate gentleman **seeks to help someone other than his self**.

№4 The ultimate gentleman **plans for success, but prepares for failure**.

№3 The ultimate gentleman **seeks wisdom over knowledge**.

№2 The ultimate gentleman is **a good provider**.

№1 The ultimate gentleman **leads by example**.

The Ultimate Gentleman's Style Guide

THE BUSINESS SUIT

The business suit is the most universally appropriate item in a gentleman's wardrobe. There are few events in which a man in a good looking suit will be out of place, particularly if the man has a firm grasp of fashion and an understanding of his personal style. A *suit* is a jacket and trousers of the same cut, made from the same fabric, and intended to be worn together. A suit adds to the existing personality of a gentleman. It is that personality that has made the suit a lasting and essential element of his wardrobe.

Different types of suits are essential in a man's wardrobe. Suits exude a style statement and profound elegance. There are various types of suits that can be worn on different occasions, therefore it is important to know and identify the different styles. Suits denote professionalism and command respect. Today, suits are worn to all formal and informal occasions.

SUIT JACKET BASICS

The first and perhaps the most noticeable element of a suit is whether the jacket is single or double-breasted. There are three types of single breasted suits; one-button, two button and three button. A single breasted suit comes with a coat or jacket having a single row of buttons and a narrow overlap of fabric. A double breasted suit has a wider overlap and two parallel rows of buttons. The two-button suit is an essential item in a gentleman's wardrobe.

The doubled breasted suit jacket is often seen as a more formal suit worn by older men for a more proper and elegant look. Unlike the single-breasted suit, the jacket of a double-breasted suit has two sets of buttons to hold the jacket closed as it wraps a little further around the waist. Double breasted suits have a slenderizing effect on portly men, while that extra panel of fabric can appear to swallow the physique of slender men.

The **One-Button** suit jacket is traditionally tailored for the lean or slim gentleman.

The **Two-Button** suit jacket is ideal for gentlemen who are average to short in height (5 foot 10 inches or less).

The **Three-Button** suit jacket is a great choice to wear to the office. It has a slightly more formal appearance.

The **doubled breasted** suit jacket is often seen as a more formal suit worn by older men for a more proper and elegant look.

OTHER SUIT STYLES

The three-piece **vested** suit is a feature of excellence in many fashion circles and is inspired by a classic look. The three-piece suit is a dressier look and is worn with a vest buttoned up underneath the suit jacket. The great thing about a three-piece suit is when you take the jacket off, you'll still look highly presentable because you're wearing a vest.

The **vest** of a three-piece suit will have either two side adjusters or the more common back adjuster.

LAWS OF THE DRESS SHIRT

A dress shirt is an essential part of a man's wardrobe. Whether it is worn every day or once a year, this single article of clothing expresses your personal style. It helps the wearer feel confident and in control during the most stressful situations. Ultimately, the fit, material, color, and style form an attractive garment that can last for years.

A proper fitting dress shirt compliments a gentleman's appearance without causing discomfort. The neck size, collar type, sleeve length, and cuff style discretely indicate whether the shirt is meant for work or for play. From a professional standpoint, men can find dress clothes for daytime conferences, client meetings, worksite supervision, or weekend catch-ups. These dress shirts cover both blue-collar and white-collar jobs, although the material choices may differ.

When a guy goes off the clock, dress shirt options open up. Men can buy dress shirts suitable for dinner with friends, first dates, late-night drinks, or formal occasions like weddings. The pattern and color of a dress shirt indicates whether someone is serious about his work or out for a good time.

The type of shirt a man wears speaks volumes about him. For instance, an ill-fitting or wrinkled dress shirt may convey that a man cares little about his appearance. On the other hand, it may indicate the presence of someone who disregards fashion rules. A blue button-down Oxford with rolled-up sleeves may signify that a guy is ready to work. A slim, white broadcloth shirt under a tailored suit may cause people to think the executive offices are within sight.

Finding the right dress shirt is not a single-step process. Just as one size does not fit all people, one shirt style or designer does not suit all men. The right dress shirt comes from a combination of fit, style (material, color, or pattern), neck size, cuff, and collar.

THE STYLE

When you are looking at dress shirts, all shirts will fall into one of three categories: Bespoke, Made-to-Measure, or Off-the-Rack.

- **Bespoke** shirts are completely custom designed for you based on a pattern drawn to fit your exact body size and preferences.

- **Made-to-Measure** shirts are modified based on a set of existing patterns to adjust for your own measurements and limited preferences.

- **Off-the-Rack** shirts are based on pre-established sizes and limited shirting fabrics, often determined by only neck and sleeve size.

THE FIT

The fit you select will depend on your body type and your personal preference. Before looking for a dress shirt, you'll need to know your size. Dress shirt sizes have two numbers: first is your neck size and the second is your sleeve length. Poor fitting shirts will be uncomfortable, so measure yourself to get an exact fit. The three major fit types are:

- **Athletic:** Also called slim or tailored, the athletic fit is the narrowest-fitting men's dress shirt.

- **Regular:** This standard dress shirt fit is a little looser than the athletic fit. If a dress shirt doesn't have a fit listed, you can assume it is regular fit.

- **Full:** The is the loosest of all dress shirt fits and is appropriate for men with a larger stature. Full-fitting men's dress shirts are also usually a little longer.

THE NECK

Dress shirt neck sizes range from 14 to 23 inches, rising in half-inch increments. To obtain the proper neck size, a man must use a flexible tape measure to measure around the neck just below the Adam's apple. Half of an inch should be added to the final distance, which is about the spacing needed to insert a finger between the neck and the collar. This gap makes the shirt feel more comfortable without choking the wearer or making him appear like he's a boy wearing his daddy's shirt.

Some shirt labels list general sizes instead of the specific neck measurement. For example, a 15-inch shirt may be listed as a medium. The following table helps to translate these size differences:

Size	Neck (Inches)	Sleeve (Inches)
S	14-14 ½	32-33
M	15-15 ½	33-34
L	16-16 ½	34-35
XL	17-17 ½	35-36
2XL	18-18 ½	36-37

Shirts with general sizing typically range from extra-small (XS), to extra-extra-extra-large (3XL). Big and Tall shirts have special design characteristics. Men who are taller than 6 feet 1 inch should concentrate on Tall sizes, which have longer shirttails and longer arms. Dress shirts for tall men end with a "T," such as MT for medium tall or LT for large tall. Men who are 6 feet 1 inch or shorter and have waist sizes larger than their chest sizes typically look best in Big sizes. These shirts range from Big 1X to Big 6X.

THE CUFF

Shirt cuffs may be a small feature, but should not be ignored. Cuffs are an important part of a shirt which defines a man's style. They are one of the few places where a gentleman's attire can be garnished with bling. The two basic cuff styles are:

- **Barrel Cuff**: This is a traditional cuff with built-in buttons. Barrel cuffs are functional and may present a modern look. Most store-bought barrel cuff shirts tend to have a single button with the corners square or angled. A dressier version of the barrel cuff has two or three buttons instead of one. Some barrel cuffed shirts are convertible, which means they have buttons but also have two holes, so you can cut off the buttons to convert the shirt to be a single cuff worn with cufflinks.

- **French Cuff**: The French cuff is the classic cuff for a dress shirt – the cuff is folded back with holes to be fastened with cufflinks instead of buttons. French cuffs are often considered more formal, particularly with the use of quality cufflinks. The French cuff is best for showing a quarter inch of shirt cuff from underneath your jacket sleeve. French cuffs can have squared, rounded or angled corners.

THE COLLAR

The basic rule of dress shirts is not to wear a collar that is the same shape as your face. Men with long, narrow faces should avoid long pointed collars. Men with round faces should avoid spread collars.

The following collars are generally accepted styles by the fashion industry. However, keep in mind that many variations exist and these rules do not apply to every man and every situation. The key is to trust your judgment and wear what makes you feel confident!

A **button-down collar** is secured to the shirt by small buttons on both points for both a stylish and practical look. The button-down collar is considered a sportier look.

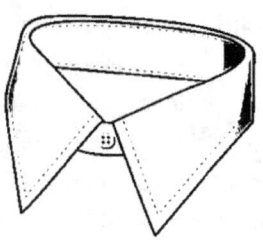

A **straight collar** is a conservative style that is flattering with any face shape. A straight collar may be worn in formal and business-casual situations. A straight collar points down and is pointed at the tips.

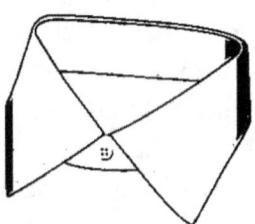

A **spread collar** is more formal than a straight collar. You may wear a tie with this collar, but consider a formal tie knot such as the Windsor knot. A spread collar has a wider angle than the straight collar.

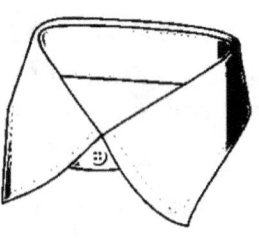

A **varsity collar** is a shorter version of the spread, updated with slightly curved lines.

BESPOKE MEN'S SHIRTS

Bespoke shirt tailoring is undergoing a surge of popularity in the United States as more men realize there are options beyond designer labels. Bespoke tailoring gives the opportunity to specify every aspect of how a shirt is cut and allows the wearer to experience the feel and look of a perfectly fitted shirt. The following is a guide on what features you should expect from a quality bespoke made men's shirt.

Obviously, the main benefit of a bespoke shirt is that it fits the wearer perfectly; after all, the shirt has been made specifically for the wearer. Signs of a bespoke shirt are:

1. The *fit* of a bespoke men's shirt should not feel tight or appear baggy across the shoulders, chest, stomach, or seat. The cut of the shirt should follow the contours of the body, without being too close or restrictive a fit. A fabric allowance of about 6 inches on the chest body measurement, 5 inches on the stomach measurement, and 6 inches on the seat measurement should give good results with average body dimensions. However, these allowances will vary depending on the wearer's build.

2. The *sleeves* of the shirt should be long enough so that the cuffs do not move up the arm when the arms are raised above the head. Similarly, they should not be so long that when the arms are hanging by the side of the body, there is significant excess of fabric on the sleeves near to the cuffs.

3. The *collar* of the shirt should leave enough space to insert your thumb comfortably between the collar and the neck when buttoned and should not feel tight or hang loose around the neck.

4. The *length* of the shirt should be long enough so that the tails hang just below the seat when worn. This will ensure that the shirt does not become untucked during use.

5. The *cuffs* of a bespoke men's shirt should be just too tight to slip over the hand when buttoned. It should be necessary to undo the cuffs when putting on the shirt.

Aside from the fit of the shirt, there are a number of other important features to keep an eye out for:

1. *Fabrics* - A bespoke men's shirt should only be constructed from pure cotton fabric. Cotton affords the wearer far greater comfort than manmade fibers and gives a classic look and feel to a shirt. The count of the fabric should be as high as possible - the higher the count, the finer the fabric. Popular fabric weaves include poplin (a plain weave and the classic English shirting), twill (a heavier, diagonal weave), fils-a-fils (a tiny graph paper check that appears to be a solid color from a distance), and oxford (generally, the heaviest weave).

2. *Collars* - The collar should be handmade and can be either fused or unfused. A well fused collar will give a smooth look with no puckering and should have cotton interfacing material. Collars should have removable collar stays to keep the shape of the wings perfectly straight when inserted.

3. *Stitching* - All stitching throughout the shirt should be single-needle stitching. This technique is more time-consuming than commercial methods, but gives strong seams that are significantly more pucker-resistant.

4. *Pattern Matching* - When using striped or patterned fabrics, pattern matching should occur wherever possible.

5. *Sleeve Plackets* - Where the sleeves meet the cuffs, traditional plackets should be used. Highest quality shirts do not provide placket buttons as these are unnecessary in a well formed placket.

6. *Split Yoke* - To ensure a perfect fit across the shoulders, a split (4 piece) yoke should be used.

7. **_Buttons_** - These should be cross-stitched onto the shirt by hand to ensure that they do not become loose over time.

8. **_Tails_** - The tails of the shirt should be rounded and strengthened by a gusset.

CHOOSING THE RIGHT TIE

It is an art to match your tie correctly with the rest of the clothes and the occasion. So how do you perfect the tricks of it? Simply remember these few guidelines.

1. Always buy the tie of correct length. Standard tie lengths are 130-150cm. Tall men should wear longer ties. An appropriate tie length is when the triangle tip of the tie touches your belt buckle.

2. Unless you can afford to buy tie widths in fashion, buy a width of 8-9cm which is a general width and will never go out of fashion.

3. When purchasing a tie to go with a suit, ensure that you carry a swatch of the suit with you. You will then have a perfect idea of how the tie will look when worn. If the jacket is a sport coat, then the color of the trousers must be taken into consideration when selecting the tie.

4. Before buying, carefully check the tie for any manufacturing defects like loose threads, uneven weaving, stains, discoloration, or smudges.

5. Casual or regular office ties can be polyester blends, but business meetings and other occasions require silks or silk blend ties.

6. For all occasions, avoid ties with pictures and cartoons. These patterns are very informal and should be worn only on informal occasions, like a birthday party or a family gathering.

7. For a job interview, business meeting, at the office or other serious occasions, the selection of a tie should be conservative. Set off a dark colored shirt or suit with a light toned tie in the same or complementing hue. Do not wear a striped tie with a striped shirt, with the exception of a pin-striped shirt. A solid tie will be a better option.

8. Match patterns and textures of the clothing with the tie. With patterned shirts, it's better to wear solid ties and vice versa. It will be a loud clash if you wear a patterned tie with a patterned shirt.

9. A dark shirt is relieved by a lighter colored tie and a bright shirt can be sobered by pairing it with a dark tie. Dark blue and dark red colors seldom go wrong in ties. You can also select a tie of the same color as your shirt or suit, but in a lighter or darker shade.

10. Your face and skin should also affect your tie selection. If you have a strong, angular face you should wear striped ties. Dotted and paisley printed ties go well with a round or baby face. Solid colors can be worn by everyone. As you would match the shirt and suit to your skin before buying, so should you follow the same principles while selecting a tie.

How to Tie a Tie

Clear illustrations and simple directions make learning how to tie a tie easy. Just review the following pages and then start practicing in front of a mirror.

FOUR IN HAND

The Four in Hand knot makes for a narrow, more discreet and slightly asymmetrical tie knot. It is best suited for a standard button-down dress shirt and works best with wide neckties made from heavy fabrics.

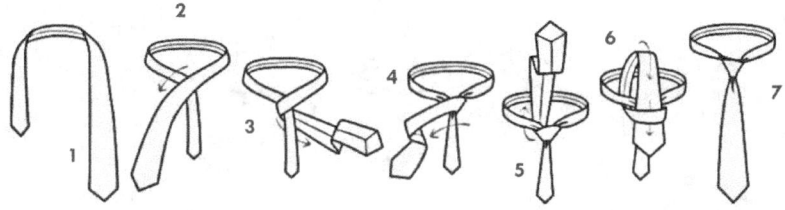

1. Start with the wide end of the tie on the right and the small end on the left. Begin with the small end slightly above your belly-button (will vary depending on your height and the length & thickness of your tie). Only move the active (wide) end.

2. Wide end over the small end to the left

3. Under the small end and to the right

4. Across the front and to the left

5. Up into the neck loop from underneath

6. Down through the loop you've just made in the front

7. Tighten the knot by pulling down on the wide end. Slide the knot up & adjust.

WINDSOR

The Windsor knot is a thick, wide and triangular tie knot that projects confidence. It would therefore be your knot of choice for presentations, job interviews, courtroom appearances etc. It is best suited for spread collar shirts and it's actually quite easy to do.

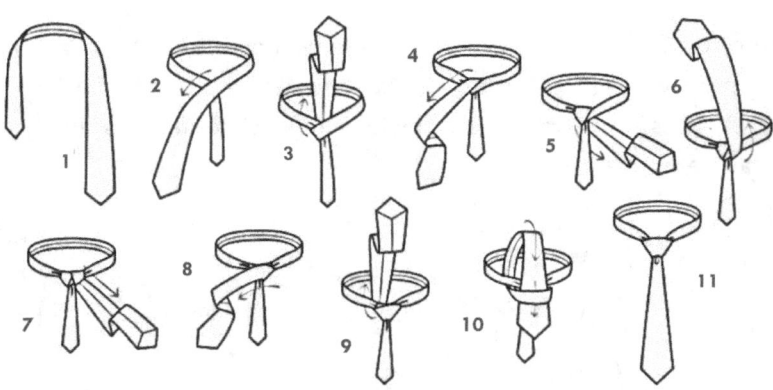

1. Start with the wide end of the tie on the right and the small end on the left. The tip of the small end should rest slightly above your belly-button (this will vary depending on your height and the length & thickness of your tie). Only move the active (wide) end.

2. Wide end over the small end to the left.

3. Up into the neck loop from underneath.

4. Down to the left.

5. Around the back of the small end to the right.

6. Up to the center, towards neck loop.

7. Through the neck loop and down to the right.

8. Across the front to the left.

9. Up into the neck loop from underneath.

10. Down through the loop you've just created in the front.

11. Tighten the knot by pulling down on the wide end. Slide the knot up & adjust.

HALF WINDSOR

The Half Windsor knot, a modest version of the Windsor knot, is a symmetrical and triangular tie knot that you can use with any dress shirt. It works best with somewhat wider neckties made from light to medium fabrics.

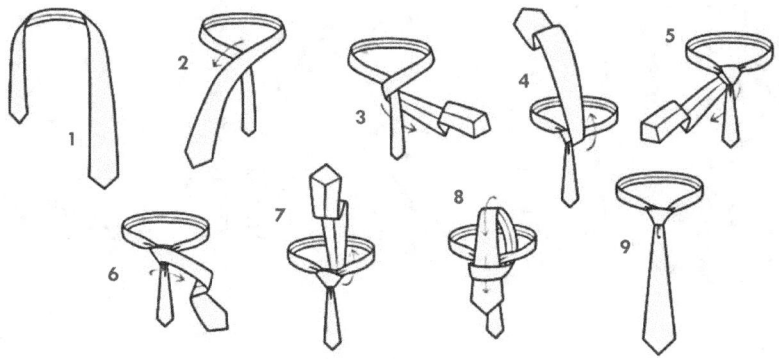

1. Start with the wide end of the tie on the right and the small end on the left. The tip of the small end should rest slightly above your belly-button (this will vary depending on your height and the length & thickness of your tie). Only move the active (wide) end.

2. Wide end over the small end to the left.

3. Under the small end and to the right.

4. Up to the center, towards neck loop.

5. Through the neck loop and to the left.

6. Across the front, over to the right.

7. Up into the neck loop from underneath.

8. Down through the loop you've just created in the front.

9. Tighten the knot by pulling down on the wide end. Slide the knot up & adjust.

BOW TIE

The Bow Tie knot is worn to give you a formal and elegant appearance. A "black tie occasion" such as a wedding is an event that you would commonly wear a bow tie at, along with a tuxedo.

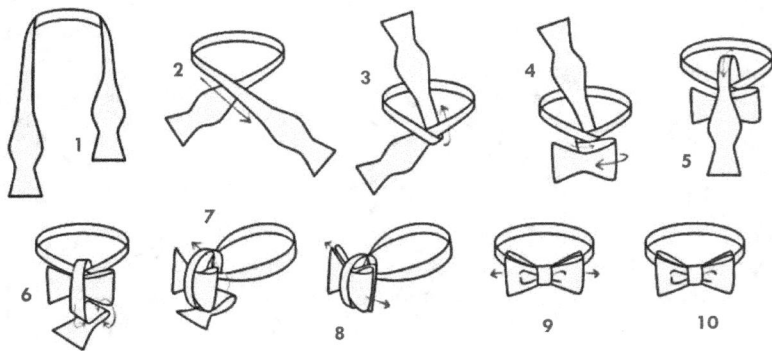

1. Start with the bowtie lying face up. Adjust the bowtie so right side is shorter than the left. The end on the left will be referred to as A and the end on the right will be referred to as B.

2. Move A to the right side, across B.

3. Bring A under B and up through the neck loop.

4. At the joint, fold B towards the right and then towards the left to create the bow shape.

5. Bring A stra-ight down over the middle of the bow shape that was made with B.

6. Fold A back towards the chest and pinch the fold.

7. Push the pinched end (A) through the loop behind B.

8. Pull on the folded parts of the bow to tighten.

9. Adjust until balanced on both sides.

10. Continue tightening the knot by pulling on the folded parts.

THE RIGHT DRESS SHOE

The first thing to consider when choosing the right dress shoe is to know what you are wearing. It seems simple, but knowing if shoes are going to be worn with business casual dress (slacks/dress shirt) as opposed to a full suit does make a difference.

With a full suit, you want the nice, traditional polish shoes to compliment the suit, as that is the look you are putting forward with wearing a suit. If you are dressing more casual, as most places are in recent times, you might consider a comfortable pair of oxfords or Rockport's. After all, if you don't have to wear full dress shoes, why not just wear a comfortable shoe.

The average person steps 4,000-5,000 times a day. That's roughly 3 miles. This can heavily impact the style of dress shoes you wear, as well as how the padding and insole are manufactured. Quality speaks for itself, as the saying goes. How well the shoes will hold up is a definite thing to consider. It's better to have two or three pairs of good shoes that will last a long time than to have fifteen pairs of generic-looking bargain brands.

How do you know what's quality?

High-quality shoes are all about construction and there are a few basic things to look for:

- Your shoes should be made of real leather and have leather soles as well. If you buy quality leather shoes, they can be refurbished a number of times and will last forever, which is ultimately going to be less expensive than having to replace crappy, poorly made shoes every few months.

- The sole of a well-made shoe will be stitched and not glued to the bottom of the shoes.

- The lining in a good pair of shoes is made of high-quality calfskin or natural leather.

- Finally, the stitching should be neat and be barely noticeable.

How do you care for your shoes?

Properly caring for your shoes is key to looking your best. Follow these tips to protect your investment and your reputation, all at the same time:

- Store them with cedar shoetrees to help draw out moisture and maintain their shape.

- Use a shoe horn to slip your shoe on rather than jamming your foot into it.

- Polish your shoes regularly to keep them looking clean and new. Having polished shoes indicates that you care about your professional appearance and pay attention to details.

- Alternate a couple pairs during the week so you don't wear them out. Even if it means you own two or three identical pairs, wear a different pair every day to prolong their lifespan.

THE ESSENTIAL TROUSERS

Trousers should not be the focal point of a man's suit. Their job is to draw the eye upward to your jacket or downward to your shoes. With that being said, the fit and design of your trousers is important. Nothing is more uncomfortable for a man than a pair of pants too tight in the crotch or too loose in the backside as to cause a draft.

FLAT FRONT VS. PLEATED

Trousers can be pleated or non-pleated (flat-front). Flat fronts compliment thin men, while pleats flatten those who are a bit larger or just prefer extra room in that area. Keep in mind that pleats often add heft to the wearer's figure and draws the eye to the midsection, while flat front pants create cleaner line and the illusion of slimness. Your decision here does have consequences – it may determine your trouser cuff decision.

Flat Front

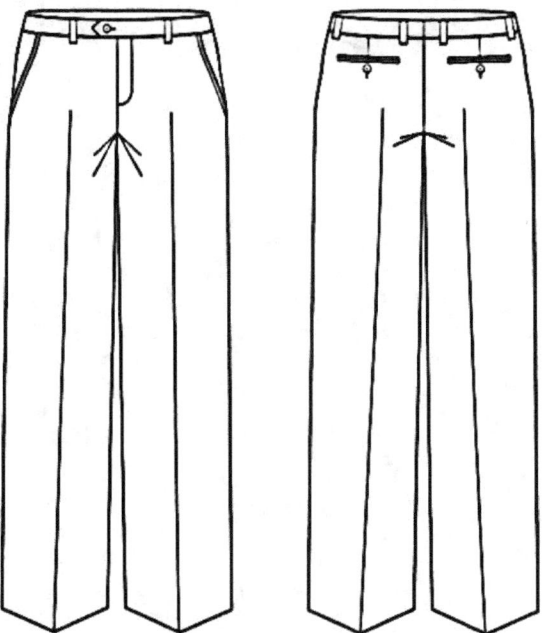

Pleated

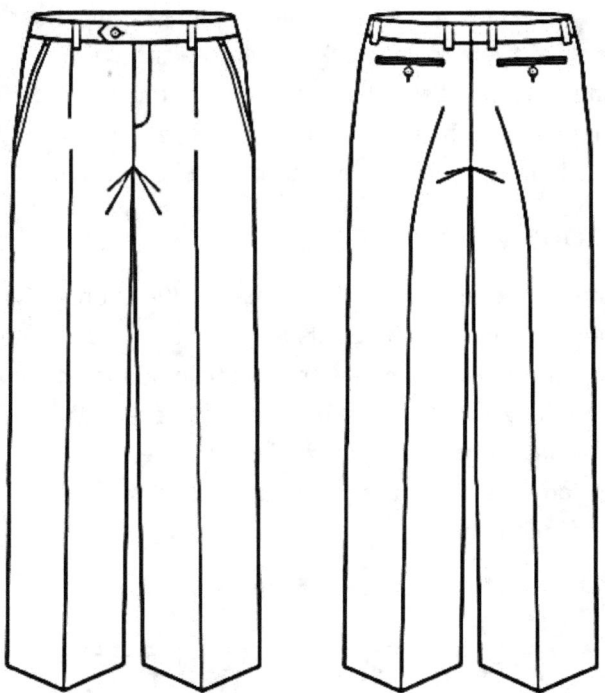

CUFFED VS UNCUFFED

Most dress pants have a small band around each ankle called "cuffs." Trouser cuffs are not a necessary embellishment, but like trouser pleats, they are often the best-looking option for most men. Trouser cuffs help add a bit of extra weight to the garment, which helps pull them straight at the bottom and keeps them from billowing about too much.

A well-fitted cuff should rest against the back of a man's shoe and drape just on top of the front of the shoe. A slightly-pointed "beak" where the pressed fold of the trouser rests on the shoe is a sign of a good fit. Cuffs also help to shorten the visual impression of a man's leg, helping the chest and face to stand out more. For this reason, shorter men may want to avoid cuffs. Some men find the unbroken line of uncuffed trousers more appealing.

Breaking these rules does not exactly constitute a glaring faux pas, but it would be an odd stylistic choice and risks drawing attention to the trousers — the opposite of their function. It's best to opt for the balanced appearance and wear unpleated trousers without cuffs; pleated trousers with them.

Basic Body Measurements

A well-dressed gentleman should know his body measurements. To determine your body measurements, use a tape measure and the help of a friend to take the following measurements. When you're done, you can easily find out your size.

- **Neck Size**
  Use the tape to measure around the base of your neck, where it meets your shoulders. Put a finger between your neck and the tape measure for a looser fit collar.

- **Chest Width**
  This measurement should be taken beneath your armpits, around the widest part of your chest and shoulder blades. Make sure to keep the tape measure horizontal, and don't pull to tight or hold your breath while measuring.

- **Sleeve**
  Bend your elbow and put your hand on your hip. Ask your friend to measure from middle of back of your neck, around your shoulder and elbow to the wrist bone.

- **Waist**
  Put the tape around your natural waistline, which should be close to your bellybutton. Put one finger between the tape and your body before you measure.

- **Inseam**
  This is measured between your groin and your lower ankle. You might find it easier to measure the inseam on a pair of pants that already fit you.

When you've taken your measurements, use the *Body Measurement Chart* on the following page to find out your clothing sizes.

BODY MEASUREMENT CHART

Size	Neck (Inches)	Chest (Inches)	Sleeve (Inches)	Waist (Inches)	Inseam (Inches)
XS	13-13 ½	32-34	32	28-30	32
S	14-14 ½	34-36	32 ½	30-32	33
M	15-15 ½	38-40	34	34-36	33
L	16-16 ½	42-44	35	38-40	34
XL	17-17 ½	46-48	35 ½	42-44	34
2XL	18-18 ½	50-52	36	46-48	34
3XL	19-19 ½	54-56	36 ½	50-52	34

Top 10 Wardrobe Accessories

Gone are the days when fashion trends were only applicable to women. Accessories are like the service and ambiance surrounding a fine meal – they add to and enrich the experience. The finest accessories in the world cannot help a man who doesn't care about his appearance; however, the proper use of them can transform a decently dressed fellow into an extraordinary dressed gentleman.

1. **Socks**
   Even though they are a timeless piece of men's fashion, socks can be a little complicated. Cotton socks have been the preferred choice for many men and the right color should be worn to complement the color of the pants.

2. **Belt**
   A high quality leather belt can last you for a long period of time. Black and brown are among the colors that can make a huge difference for those who want to stand out in the crowd. These colors are fantastic because they can easily match well with all your suits.

3. **Collar Stays**
   Collar stays get bent out of shape and often need replacing. They keep the shirt collar in place by adding weight and crispness to an otherwise light and flexible piece of fabric. Collar stays are small details that make your dress shirt collar points look crisp.

4. **Pocket Squares**
   All men should invest in pocket squares that are linen or silk. When matching a pocket square with your tie, make sure they are not from the same material; for example, don't wear a silk tie and silk pocket square.

5. **Cuff Links**
   Cufflinks offer a professional and classic look. People know you mean business when you are wearing a pair. There are many

cufflink designs to choose from and are made from many different kinds of material.

6. **Tie Bar**

The tie bar and its cousins are a great example of an accessory that serves a purpose. It keeps your tie from flying over your shoulder on a windy day and from falling into your food at a meal. Tie bars can also add a bit of pizzazz to an otherwise dull ensemble. It can be a simple stripe of gold, silver, or some other metal. Other variations to the tie bar include the tie chain and the tie tack.

7. **Scarf**

Many men think that a scarf is just for women, but this is not always the case. Invest in a high quality scarf and wear it during the winter to keep you warm and looking stylish. It can be paired with a pea coat or a casual jacket.

8. **The Boutonnière**

A boutonnière is a floral decoration worn by men, typically a single flower or bud. Boutonnière is the French word for "buttonhole". A boutonnière is the simplest, least used and most perfect accessory a man can add to compliment his clothing. It requires strength to wear, it doesn't last long, it has a storied history and on a spring day it can be found for free. A boutonnière is properly worn on the left breast near the heart. Keeping it simple and subtle is the key to pulling it off.

9. **Messenger Bags**

The days of the brief case are played out. Stylish messenger bags for men compliment great looking attire. They show a sign of elegance and can be used to carry any number of items. The best thing with men's messenger bags is that they are available in many colors and sizes.

10. **Top Coat**

You should always invest in a quality top coat. A good top coat will serve you for years. Buy a classic looking coat or a pea coat. If you can afford it, get yourself a good trench coat.

The Ultimate Gentleman's Lifestyle Guide

10 THINGS A MAN SHOULD LEARN BEFORE 25

There are specific things every man should learn regardless of his status as a gentleman. This doesn't mean you should be a know-it-all, however you want to have basic survival, professional and interpersonal skills to use throughout life. Here are 10 suggested things every man should learn before he reaches 25 years old.

1. **How to Drive a Manual**
   Knowing how to drive a manual transmission car means you will better understand how any vehicle works. Being in the right gear for the situation you're in is very important whether driving an automatic or manual car.

2. **How to Replace a Flat Tire**
   A gentleman should know how to replace a flat tire. If you've never replaced a tire, practice this skill by removing and replacing an existing healthy tire. Having some practice under your belt can make changing a tire on a busy road a little less frustrating.

3. **How to Build a Fire**
   In many survival situations, the ability to start a fire can make the difference between living and dying. Fire can fulfill many needs. You can use fire to purify water, sterilize bandages, signal for rescue, and provide protection from animals. In an emergency situation a fire can be a psychological boost by providing peace of mind and companionship. You can also use fire to produce tools and weapons.

4. **How to Perform CPR**

Cardiopulmonary Resuscitation (CPR) is a combination of rescue breathing and chest compressions delivered to victims thought to be in cardiac arrest. By knowing this life-saving technique, you will have the power to save a life. Statistics show that immediate CPR can more than double a victim's chance of survival.

5. **How to Negotiate**

Negotiating is something that most people don't like to do. If you know how to negotiate you can save yourself a lot of money. Your ability to negotiate is key to both your personal and business success. You can always get a better deal if you know how to improve your interpersonal skills. You never need to settle for less or feel dissatisfied with the result of any negotiation. The secret to negotiating is to understand that there is almost always a way to get better terms or prices, whether you are a buyer or seller. Your job is to find that way.

6. **How to Swim**

Swimming is a valuable skill, but is best learned as a child for a variety of reasons. Many people that don't learn to swim as a child develop a fear of the water. Not only do they never want to swim, they become dangerous to other swimmers around them. If in distress, an inexperienced swimmer may pull another swimmer under water to save themselves. Swimming is important for fitness and is one activity that can be done throughout the lifespan. Since swimming is done in the water there is minimal impact on the joints.

7. **How to Speak a Foreign Language**

Our world is getting smaller and learning a foreign language is more important than ever. Most people outside the United States can speak more than one language; their native tongue and English. When you speak only one language you subjugate yourself to being shut out from a global economy. If your resume shows that you are multi-lingual, more often than not, you will be chosen over other prospective employees that speak only one language.

8. **Speaking in Public**
    Many people are terrified of speaking in public or in front of a group. However, becoming a good public speaker will give you confidence in many areas of your life. In many ways it can help you advance your career. Most people who advance in their job or business find that often they have to give speeches or presentations. To get started, read some books on public speaking or attend some workshops. The best way to jump start your public speaking is to just do it. Begin speaking at parties, church or family gatherings. Simply put, just start!

9. **How to Ask for Help**
    Asking for help creates an atmosphere of empowerment. It communicates to others that, while you may not have the answers, you are willing to find them and make things better. Successful people are driven and motivated — and when the going gets tough, the tough ask for help!

10. **How to Cook**
    Learning to cook is a good way to impress and show your appreciation to loved ones. You don't have to be a professional chef in order to serve a wonderful meal. Men who can cook are more grown-up, responsible, and independent. Being able to cook is a lifetime skill. Having learned to cook, you will never have to be dependent on anyone else for a great meal.

20 THINGS A MAN CAN TEACH A BOY...

...that can help him become a good man!

1. How to get up after falling down.

2. Trust is earned, not given.

3. Working smarter over working harder.

4. Physical fitness and competition are important.

5. Give everything you do 110% effort.

6. Your word is your bond!

7. Excuses are useless.

8. All men are not "dogs". Show him a good man!

9. Thinking BIG!

10. The difference between getting hurt and being injured.

11. There are no trophies handed out for being a good man, it's your job!

12. He is a born leader.

13. Faith in God.

14. Not to talk too much.

15. How to leave home.

16. What a good woman looks and acts like!

17. The word "no" means "no".

18. Not to work for money, but to make money work for you.

19. Boys don't pee sitting down!

20. He is not a man, until he becomes one.

A Gentleman's Toolkit

Men often get lost in the shuffle on what they should purchase when it comes to products. The following items are essential products that are necessary for every gentleman's personal toolkit.

- **Breath Mints**
  A small pocket sized pack of breath mints should be an essential part of every man's tool kit. A hearty lunch could impart a nasty aroma to your breath, particularly if you've been eating garlic or onions. Having breath mints on hand will help alleviate bad breath.

- **A Good Razor**
  All you need is a good razor with a fresh, sharp blade. The multi-blade cartridge razors are great, but you can still get a great shave with a disposable one. One of the most important factors in a gentleman's appearance is his shave. A good shave makes a man look well groomed, clean, younger, and have much better facial features including clearer skin.

- **Exfoliator**
  Exfoliates work by scraping away dead skin cells from your face (or body) leaving you with a bright new layer of skin. It also helps unclog your pores and reduce acne breakouts. Use an exfoliate at least once a month but no more than a couple of times per week.

- **Facial Moisturizer**
  A facial moisturizer is the most popular product among men's grooming products. Shaving can often irritate the pores of your skin. One of the basic grooming tips is to apply moisturizer daily to protect your skin's pores.

- **Hand Cream**
  Hand cream helps keep the skin on your hands smooth, which means they'll look younger and feel softer to touch. Rub your

hands with cream after they come in contact with soap or other products that dry out your skin.

- **Lip Balm**
  Lips are especially sensitive to environmental conditions. Dry and chapped lips are more prone to cold sores and infections, which in addition to not being healthy; they don't look real attractive either. Using lip balm will keep your lips lubricated and delay the appearance of age-related lines.

- **A Money Clip**
  For the gentleman who carries cash, it might make sense to use a money clip to replace a bulky wallet. Use a money clip to carry bills, an ID and a couple of credit cards. Money clips can reduce pocket congestion and allow you to carry cash safely in places where a wallet can't fit. Stashing a money clip in your front pocket rather than in the back also discourages thieves and pickpockets. A money clip also helps eliminate the overstuffed wallet effect.

- **A Planner/Organizer**
  Planners are essential tools for time management. A variety of good tools are available to help you with time management. A daily planner enables you to record your tasks on a predefined calendar. Usually, a planner has entry points for 24 hours a day, allowing you to add task at any hour on any day. Daily planners are available in different formats: paper or digital (computer and mobile phone) based.

- **Quality Cologne**
  An essential grooming product is cologne. Whether it is a body spray or a more refined perfume, every gentleman should have it in his tool kit. When picking a scent, one of the first things to consider is personal style and image. Try a few different scents and figure out what impression each one gives and if it's true to your own style. The key to a good first impression may very well rest in how well you smell.

- **Shaving Cream**
  Shaving cream facilitates a better shave by reducing the chances of razor burn. It is applied to the face in order to lubricate your skin and hair. Shaving cream may come in the form of a gel, oil or foam. It can be purchased in tubs, bars, cans and squeezable tubes.

- **Sunscreen**
  No matter what the weather is like, men should apply sunscreen every day. Doing so in the AM will prevent solar radiation and damaging rays from reaching your skin, preventing potential sun burn.

- **Swiss Army Knife**
  A Swiss Army knife or multi-tool gives you the basic ability to fix and open a wide variety of things, without having to carry a tool box or tool belt around with you.

- **Timepiece (Watch)**
  Few things say more about a man than his watch. Its character, look and style can give others a peek into a man's background (and priorities) without having to ask a single question. That is why purchasing a watch is such a personal and important decision.

- **Writing Instrument (Pen)**
  A good pen can do wonders for your image and will make writing more pleasurable. You can buy a quality Parker or Sheaffer pen for as little as $20. You could spend more and get a fountain pen, but they require more maintenance and you run the risk of the ink leaking and damaging your clothing. A decent refillable roller ball pen is all you need.

17 BOOKS EVERY MAN SHOULD READ

I have identified a list of fiction and non-fiction books that I strongly recommend for men to read.

It goes without saying that well-read men often have superior intellect in comparison to men who just look at the pictures. Here are the top 17 books that I think every man must read, regardless of whether you read a lot or a little.

1. **Who Moved My Cheese,** *by Dr. Spencer Johnson*
    This simple book has a dramatically important message about how to cope with change. People fear change because they believe they cannot control how or when it happens to them. What matters most is the attitude we have about change and how we react and deal with it when it comes.

2. **The Secrets Men Keep**, *by Stephen Arteburn*
    Secrets are the most dangerous force within a man. Finding a way to deal with the unspoken fears and questions that threaten to undo you is among your most important tasks.

3. **The Souls of Black Folk,** *by W.E.B. Dubois*
    Essential reading for everyone interested in African-American history and the struggle for civil rights in America.

4. **Oh, The Places You'll Go,** *by Dr. Suess*
    Dr. Seuss addresses life's ups and downs with his trademark humorous verse and illustrations, while encouraging readers to find the success that lies within.

5. **The Decline and Fall of the Roman Empire,** *by Edward Gibbon*
    Among the most magnificent and ambitious narratives in European literature. Its subject is the fate of one of the world's greatest civilizations over thirteen centuries – its rulers, wars, society, and the events that led to its disastrous collapse.

6. **Holy Bible,** *Inspired by the Word of God*
    The Bible is literally "God-breathed" (2 Timothy 3:16). In other words, it is God's very words to us. There are so many questions

that philosophers have asked that God answers for us in Scripture. What is the purpose to life? Where did I come from? Is there life after death? How do I get to heaven? Why is the world full of evil? Why do I struggle to do good?

7. **The Art of War,** *by Sun Tzu*
One of the most influential books of military strategy ever written. This classic of Chinese philosophy lays out a systematic, rational approach to tactics and strategy that leaders worldwide have applied not only to the military, but also to business, law, martial arts, and sports.

8. **The Known World,** *by Edward P. Jones*
Edward Jones has woven a footnote of history into an epic that takes an unflinching look at slavery in all its moral complexities. Set in antebellum Virginia, it examines the issues regarding the ownership of black slaves by both white and black Americans.

9. **Legends of the Fall,** *by Jim Harrison*
This powerful story explores the theme of revenge and the actions to which people resort when their lives or goals are threatened, painting an unforgettable portrait of the twentieth-century man.

10. **Revolutionary Road,** *by Richard Gates*
The most evocative portrayal of the opulent desolation of the American suburbs. It's the story of a bright, beautiful, and talented couple who have lived on the assumption that greatness is only just around the corner. With heartbreaking compassion and remorseless clarity, this book shows how this couple mortgages their spiritual birthright, betraying not only each other, but their best selves.

11. **Moby Dick,** *by Herman Melville*
Considered an outstanding work of Romanticism and the American Renaissance. A sailor called Ishmael narrates the obsessive quest of Ahab, captain of the whaler Pequod, for

revenge on Moby Dick, a white whale which on a previous voyage destroyed Ahab's ship and severed his leg at the knee.

12. **The 5 Love Languages,** *by Dr. Gary Chapman*
You'll discover the secret that has transformed millions of relationships worldwide. Whether your relationship is flourishing or failing, this book reveals a proven approach to showing and receiving love. It will help you experience deeper and richer levels of intimacy with your partner-starting today.

13. **The Call of the Wild,** *by Jack London*
The book opens at a ranch in the Santa Clara Valley of California when a dog named Buck is stolen from his home and sold into service as a sled dog in Alaska. He progressively reverts to a wild state in the harsh climate, where he is forced to fight to dominate other dogs. By the end, he sheds the veneer of civilization and relies on primordial instinct and learned experience to emerge as a leader in the wild.

14. **Rich Dad, Poor Dad,** *by Robert Kiyosaki*
This book explodes the myth that you need to earn a high income to be rich and explains the difference between working for money and having your money work for you.

15. **A Good Man to a Valiant Man,** *by Allen Meyer*
This book is a call for valiant men to rebuild the moral walls in their hearts, to renew the thought patterns in their minds, and to take responsibility for the emotional and spiritual health of their families: the kind of men that women and children can depend on.

16. **7 Habits of Highly Effective People,** *by Stephen Covey*
This book presents a holistic, integrated, principle-centered approach for solving personal and professional problems. Covey reveals a step-by-step pathway for living with fairness, integrity, service, and human dignity – principles that give us the security to adapt to change and the wisdom and power to take advantage of the opportunities that change creates.

17. **Power of Positive Thinking,** *by Norman Vincent Peale*
    This bestseller was written with the sole objective of helping the reader achieve a happy, satisfying, and worthwhile life," Dr. Peale demonstrates the power of faith in action. With the practical techniques outlined in this book, you can energize your life and give yourself the initiative needed to carry out your ambitions and hopes.

7 Ways to Make a Great First Impression

Anyone who wants to make a great first impression needs a set of ground rules for behavior. Whether at an important job interview, having lunch with colleagues or entertaining influential clients, how you conduct yourself may make or break your career. Here are 7 ways to make a lasting impression in any professional setting.

1. **Always introduce yourself.**
    Introduce yourself to others whenever the opportunity arises, unless you already know them. It makes people feel valued regardless of their status or position.

2. **Give a firm handshake.**
    Not only does this simple gesture demonstrate that you're polite, confident and approachable, it also sets the tone for any potential future professional relationships. In a very casual work atmosphere you might be able to get away with a nod or a hello, but it's worth it to make the extra effort to offer your hand.

3. **Use appropriate manners.**
    Always say "please" and "thank you." Today, sending a thank you e-mail is perfectly acceptable, but a handwritten thank you note is always a nice touch.

4. **Watch your language.**
    Verbal and written communication are often much less formal than in times past, but be careful to choose your words wisely. Of course, derogatory, rude or offensive language is unacceptable, but so is slang. While it may be commonplace in our society, it's never acceptable in a professional atmosphere.

5. **Acknowledge others.**
    When someone approaches you, acknowledge him or her. If you're in the middle of something important, it's fine to ask them to wait a minute while you finish. If you pass someone in the hallway or on the street, but don't have time to talk, at least

wave a hand and say hello. Busyness is not an excuse to ignore people.

6. **Don't be a business card pusher.**
Don't simply hand out business cards to everyone you meet. It's a bit aggressive unless you're on a sales call. Ask for the other person's card, offer to exchange cards or ask if you can leave your card before you reach in your pocket.

7. **Show genuine interest.**
Keep eye contact and make an effort to truly listen to what others are saying. We are so easily distracted in this climate of increasingly short attention spans; we often can't wait for the other person to hurry up and finish so we can move on to the next thing. Resist the lure of distraction and haste. Take the time to ask questions and show an interest in the other person's thoughts.

15 THINGS EVERY MAN MUST DO WITHIN HIS LIFETIME

Apart from career, education, or family, a man's to do list often neglects life experiences. While it is good to have big things on your check list, it is also important not to miss out on some other equally important things which we tend to ignore. Most men get so caught in the busyness of the daily grind, that we never really explore the endless possibilities life has to offer.

Here are 15 things every man must experience at least once in his life to help him evolve as a person.

1. **Grow a beard.** It'll make you look more masculine, distinguished, and intellectual.

2. **Experience death.** Grief is something we'll all go through at least once in our lives. It will show you how strong you really are.

3. **Quit a bad habit.** It takes a lot of courage to give up a bad habit. Only a real man can do this. There is nothing better than conquering something that controls your day-to-day activities.

4. **Experience winning.** We're all average in most things we do. At least once in your life feel the high of being the best one even if for a moment.

5. **Have children.** Children will make you happier. There is something about the love a parent has for their child that is different than all other loves.

6. **Have your heart broken.** Heartbreaks may be devastating, but they always teach you a thing or two. Life moves on and there's no better of way of realizing it than getting your heart broken.

7. **Live by yourself.** Nothing makes you wiser than living completely by yourself. While you're young, move out. Even if for a short time, a man should live on his own. It'll make a man out of you.

8. **Take a road trip.** At least one road trip before you hit your thirties is a must. It is a completely different experience from the regular destination vacations you've been going on your entire life. So, hop into your car and set out on a life-altering journey with your best buds!

9. **Forgive someone.** "Forgiveness is not always easy. At times, it feels more painful than the wound we suffered, to forgive the one that inflicted it. And yet, there is no peace without forgiveness." *Marianne Williamson*

10. **Volunteer.** Start a petition. Contribute to an organization. Raise awareness of a problem. Don't be a bystander to injustice and evil.

11. **Learn to play chess.** It's the game of Kings and it doesn't take long to learn. It does take a lifetime to be really good. Knowing how to play will always make you a better man.

12. **Stand up for someone else.** It could be just shutting down gossip, speaking out against injustice or participating in worthwhile cause. "If you don't stand for something you will fall for anything." *Peter Marshall*

13. **Experience failure.** Fail at least once. Failure is as life-changing as success, probably even more. Don't be afraid to lose. Failure will only make you stronger. Until you know failure, you won't be able to appreciate success. Those who hit rock bottom and make their way back up, become legends.

14. **Conquer your fears.** Everyone needs to know fear and more importantly, what it feels like to conquer it. You must do at least one thing that scares you out of your mind. You will see yourself emerging braver and stronger. Conquer your fears. Evolve.

15. **Start a business.** Do something as simple as selling on eBay. Working for yourself or making your own money gives an incomparable sense of freedom.

GIVING HER THE ULTIMATE FLOWER

What's the best way for a man to make a lasting impression on a woman? The answer to making a memorable impact is through flowers. Studies show that 92% of women can remember the last time they received flowers and 89% say receiving flowers makes them feel special.

If the way to a man's heart is through his stomach, then the pathway to a woman's heart is through her senses. Flowers have long been used to convey our innermost feelings. Say it with flowers and you have a good chance of declaring your undying love and devotion to the woman of your dreams.

The ultimate gentleman's flower of choice is a "rose". Roses are the ultimate flower for expression of emotion or feeling. As a gift, roses can convey different meanings if the person receiving them knows the symbolism attached to the various colors. Here is the message you are sending based on the color and type of flower you choose.

1. *Red* signifies love and passion. True red is the flower for lovers.

2. *Yellow* roses once meant jealousy, but today the color signifies friendship, familiar love, and domestic happiness.

3. *Pink* flowers signify elegance, gentility, and poetic romance, without the seriousness signified by red.

4. *White* roses are sometimes called the "flower of light" and are the bride's flower. They symbolize unity, sincerity, loyalty, purity, and a love stronger than death.

5. *Purple* roses represent majestic glory and can symbolize eternal love, while lavender or lilac signifies love at first sight or the beginning of true feelings.

6. *Black* roses are symbolic of death. Many people view flowers of this color as an omen, but they can signify change or rejuvenation on the horizon, as some buds appear black but then bloom into crimson red.

Many flower colors come in various shades, which can signify slightly different meanings from their primary colors. Mixing different colors together in one bouquet is an excellent way to convey a mixture of emotions when one sentiment is not enough.

10 Signs She May Become your Wife

Throughout most of this book I talk about the traits and characteristics of men. However, I get a little nervous when I talk about the traits and characteristics of women. Here are 10 ways to know that the lady you're with is the one you should marry.

1. **She is an intellectual challenge.**
    If you want to spend the rest of your life with a woman, it is important that you find her intellectually challenging. Looks are deceiving, but personality is forever. Your conversations together should be interesting, insightful and full of depth. Your lady should be able to challenge your opinions, opening up your mind to new ideas and concepts.

2. **She is emotionally stable.**
    The woman you choose to marry should be stable emotionally. If you struggle to predict her mood and responses, you may find yourself carrying the burden of her emotions. She shouldn't transform into a more difficult person after a few months together; she should be fully honest about her feelings and emotional state.

3. **She is empathetic.**
    If you think she's the one, then make sure she is compassionate and supportive towards others and their struggles. You will have days when you are down or upset. Your wife should be the main one supporting and relating to you during these times.

4. **She is honest.**
    Honesty is a very important trait in a long-term relationship. If you can't trust your lady, how can you tell her anything in confidence or believe anything she says to you? Find someone who respects you enough to be honest with you, even when it is difficult for them.

5. **She has ambition.**

   As well as supporting your dreams and goals, the lady you marry should have her own dreams and ambitions. She plans for the future and how to improve her life. She can be independent yet willing to share and involve you in her success.

6. **She has similar values.**

   More often than not, our value system comes from our family upbringing. The things we find important (or not), the things we believe in strongly (or not), the way we treat others and ourselves can be huge factors in a relationship. It doesn't matter how attracted you are to someone or even how well you get along, if your values don't align, you will always clash in the long term.

7. **She's not petty or jealous.**

   Some jealously is natural in relationships, but the woman you marry should be secure enough in herself and you to know she doesn't need to feel jealous. This also has a lot to do with trust; she should be able to trust you enough to give you your freedom.

8. **She is giving.**

   A healthy, stable relationship focuses on giving rather than receiving. Seeing your lady happy should make you just as happy. Your joy should be her joy—it can be as simple as asking about your day or looking after you when you are sick. As time passes, the excitement at the beginning of the relationship will pass. However, both of you should be focused on meeting each other's needs.

9. **She inspires you.**

   Your lady's actions and her attitude should motivate you to be a better version of yourself. Even if she goes to the gym regularly or volunteers with a charity, you should be encouraged enough by her to be the best man you can be. A good woman will empower those around her. She will strive for greatness and therefore inspire others to strive for it as well.

10. **She can cook or at least wants to learn.**

    The woman you marry loves not only to cook, but chooses delicious and healthy meals. The way to a man's heart is through his stomach after all, right?

REAL MEN COOK

Men today have made cooking a part of their normal repertoire. Learning to cook can be an excellent way for a man to express his love towards his closest friends and family. You don't have to be a professional chef in order to serve a wonderful meal.

I strongly believe that men should learn to cook because:

- Being able to cook is a lifetime skill. Having learned to cook, you will never have to be dependent on fast food. It's unhealthy to buy fast-food, and is costlier — especially when on a tight budget. Instead, he can easily whip up something simple yet nutritious.

- Men who can cook are more grown-up, responsible, and independent.

- Cooking is also a fun thing for couples to do together. It's a good time to get your hands dirty, do something creative and then enjoy the results together afterwards.

- Cooking is one of the easiest ways to improve your diet and stick to reasonable portions.

- Cooking is relaxing, fun, creative, purposeful and hopefully delicious.

Dining Etiquette

Etiquette affects almost every aspect of dining. Dining etiquette rules apply before you ever take your seat and continue after you excuse yourself from the table. Even if you think you have impeccable manners, the tips below can help you make a better impression during your next business dinner.

- Always chew and swallow all the food in your mouth before taking in more or taking a drink.

- When eating rolls, break off a piece of bread before buttering. Eating it whole looks tacky.

- Never lick or put your knife in your mouth.

- Never chew with your mouth open. No one wants to see food being chewed or hearing it being chomped on.

- It is impolite to have your elbows on the table while you are eating.

- Don't reach over someone's plate for something; ask for the item to be passed.

- Never use your fingers to push food onto your spoon or fork.

- It is impolite to slurp your food or eat noisily.

- Never blow your nose on a napkin. Napkins are for dabbing your lips only.

- Never take food from your neighbors' plate.

- Never pick food out of your teeth with your fingernails.

THE TABLE SETTING

Sitting down for dinner at a properly set table can be a little anxiety inducing. What fork to use first? Is this the dessert spoon or the soup spoon? Even more challenging can be if you are asked to set the table for a formal dinner.

Many people are a bit confused about how to arrange the silverware and other items. Understanding a few basics of table setting can take the mystery out of this age-old custom.

Understanding the basics of table setting will show your dinner guest how sophisticated and cultured you are when sitting down for a formal meal. Here are some things to remember.

- Always work from the outside in. That means that the fork on the extreme outside will be the one used for the first course and the same applies to glassware and cutlery.

- Forks appear on the left of the dishes and knives on the right. If a soup spoon is being used, it will be on the far right of the knives.

- Dessert silverware appears above the place setting. The fork prongs will be facing to the right. The dessert spoon will be facing to the left.

- The napkin will be placed on the far left, unless a decorative napkin fold is used. Then the napkin may be placed where the hostess decides.

- If bread and butter will be served, a separate plate and butter knife will be on the table at the top left.

- Plates are stacked according to service. The main course plate will be at the bottom; salad, appetizer and soup bowl will be stacked accordingly on top.

- In terms of beverage glasses, generally the water glass is the largest-rimmed glass and is to the left, while being placed on the right side of the table setting. White wine and red wine glasses will be alongside it.

For those who need some visual assistance, use the diagram on the following page for direction.

TABLE SETTING

The Ultimate Gentleman's Personality

7 STYLE CHARACTERISTICS OF A MAN

Every gentleman has a different and unique style. Your style – a preference for behaving one way rather than another – governs the way you lead, work, communicate, make decisions, and manage change. It even governs the way you dress and how you spend your free time. From the **aficionado** to **sophisticate**, find out which of the seven style characteristics fits you.

1. **Adventurous**

   The *adventurous* man enjoys or seeks adventure. He is also friendly, adaptable, and action-oriented. His clothing choice includes canvass or wool jackets, denim jeans, and work boots. He owns a motorcycle and/or muscle car. The adventurer spends his free time traveling and playing sports.

2. **Aficionado**

   The *aficionado* man is very knowledgeable and enthusiastic about an activity, subject, or pastime. His clothing choices include tailored blazers and dress shirts. He may own several expensive watches and has a designer suit closet. The aficionado enjoys puffing a fine cigar and collecting classic sports cars.

3. **Connoisseur**

   The *connoisseur* man is especially competent to pass critical judgments in an art, particularly in matters of taste or the fine arts. His clothing choices include double breasted blazers and pressed trousers. He will usually have a wine cellar in his home. The connoisseur spends his free time painting, cooking or entertaining guest.

4. **Executive**

   The *executive* man has senior managerial responsibility in a business organization. His clothing item of choice is a "power suit". He may have a large suit and shoe collection. The executive spends his free time making money and playing golf.

5. **Intellectual**

   The *intellectual* man is a logical, original, and creative thinker. He can become very excited about theories and ideas. His clothing choices include tweed blazers, no wrinkle khaki pants, and button down oxford shirts. He owns an extensive book collection. The intellectual enjoys teaching others and solving problems.

6. **Professional**

   The *professional* man is often driven by career success and upward corporate mobility. He may work in the IT, sales or marketing career fields. His clothing choices include lightweight suits, slim-fit shirts, and dark neckties. He spends his free time managing his personal financial portfolio and working out at the gym.

7. **Sophisticated**

   The *sophisticated* man has a lot of knowledge about the world, including culture, art, and literature. He is a sophisticated person. His clothing choices include soft-shouldered tailoring, colorful accessories and slip on dress shoes. He owns land and spends his free time buying and selling fine art.

THE PERSONALITY QUIZ

The Ultimate Gentleman's Personality Quiz will help you identify your personality type and match it with a color. This model of categorizing personality style is based on many years of work by researchers and psychologists. Essentially, this quiz draws heavily on the work of Isabel Briggs-Myers, Katherine Briggs, and David Keirsey. Don Lowry, a student of Keirsey, developed the system called True Colors, which uses four primary colors to designate personality types and behavioral styles.

The True Colors program was designed to maximize the application of psychological style in the workplace, in the family, in education and in other types of communities. The ease of understanding and use in all human relationships and interactions, make True Colors very functional. The belief is that with increased understanding of ourselves and others that conflict will decrease.

Each color is associated with certain personality traits or behaviors. Everyone has some degree of each color, but one color is dominant. Identifying your personality using True Colors provides you with insight into different motivations, actions and communication approaches.

True Colors works because it is based on true principles and is easy to remember and use. It can be valuable in all kinds of circumstances from personal relationships to professional preparedness.

Follow the instructions carefully and score yourself on the following page. If you have two colors with the same score, pick the one you think more accurately describes you.

PERSONALITY QUIZ INSTRUCTIONS

In the following boxes, there are groups of word clusters printed horizontally in rows. Look at all the choices in the first box (A, B, C, D). Read the words and decide which of the four letter choices are most like you. Give that a "4". Then rank order the next three letter choices from 3-1 in descending preference. You will end up with a box of four letter choices, ranked from "4" (most like you) to "1" (least like you). Continue this process with the remaining four boxes until each have 4, 3, 2, and 1.

Box One			
A ☐	B ☐	C ☐	D ☐
active opportunistic spontaneous	parental traditional responsible	authentic harmonious compassionate	versatile inventive competent

Box Two			
E ☐	F ☐	G ☐	H ☐
curious conceptual knowledgeable	unique empathetic communicative	practical sensible dependable	competitive impetuous impactful

Box Three			
I ☐	J ☐	K ☐	L ☐
loyal conservative organized	devoted warm poetic	realistic open-minded adventuresome	theoretical seeking ingenious

Box Four			
M ☐	N ☐	O ☐	P ☐
concerned procedural cooperative	daring impulsive fun	tender inspirational dramatic	determined complex composed

Box Five			
Q ☐	R ☐	S ☐	T ☐
philosophical principled rational	vivacious affectionate sympathetic	exciting courageous skillful	orderly conventional caring

YOUR PERSONALITY SCORE

Total up your scores in the box below. If any of your scores in the boxes below are less than 5 or greater than 20 you have made an error.

TOTAL	TOTAL	TOTAL	TOTAL
A, H, K, N, S	B, G, I, M, T	C, F, J, O, R	D, E, L, P, Q
☐	☐	☐	☐
ORANGE	**GOLD**	**BLUE**	**GREEN**

Now that you have scored your personality; write the color of your personality below.

My Brightest Color Is
(The color of your highest total.)

_____

Shaded With
(The color of your second highest total.)

_____

And
(The color of your second lowest total.)

_____

With a Pale
(The color of your lowest total.)

_____

WHAT DOES IT ALL MEAN?

ORANGE: Your strength is **Skillfulness**
You are a gentleman who needs freedom to take immediate action! You have a zest for life and a desire to test the limits. You take pride in being highly skilled in a variety of fields. You are a master negotiator. Adventure is your middle name. You prefer a hands-on approach to problem solving and a direct line of reasoning creates the excitement and immediate results that you admire.

GOLD: Your strength is **Duty**
You are a gentleman who values order and cherishes the traditions of home and family. You provide for and support the structure of society. Steadfastness and loyalty are your trademarks. Generous and parental by nature, you show you care by making everyone do the right thing. To disregard responsibility of any kind never occurs to you.

BLUE: Your strength is **Authenticity**
You are a gentleman who seeks to express the inner you. Authenticity and honesty are valued above all other characteristics. You are sensitive to subtlety and - with great flair - you create roles in life's drama. You enjoy close relationships with those you love and you possess a strong spirituality in your nature. Making a difference in the world is easy for you because you cultivate the potential in yourself and in others.

GREEN: Your Strength Is **Knowledge**
You are a gentleman who feels best about yourself when you are solving problems and when your ideas are recognized, especially when you feel ingenious. You seek to express yourself through your ability to be an expert in everything. Your idea of a great day is to use your know-how like a laser to create solutions, in that you are a complex individualist with great analytical ability. Although you do not express your emotions openly, you do experience deep feelings.

The Ultimate Gentleman's Glossary

FASHION ESSENTIALS

100's Two-Ply Broadcloth (fine)
A premium shirt fabric made with two-ply threads (two individual threads are twisted together) which make it durable, soft, and lustrous.

140's Broadcloth (very fine)
A very luxurious yarn with a high thread count and close weave. This gives it a superior texture and remarkable shine.

200's Two-Ply Broadcloth (extremely fine)
This cloth is woven from some of the finest cottons in the world. The 200's Two-Ply broadcloth offers an extremely silky touch and incredibly fine patterns.

Argyle
Argyle designs are common in sweaters and socks. It is composed of an intarsia knit (see Intarsia Knit) characterized by colored diamond shapes.

Bespoke
The art of making something entirely to the buyer's preference and specification. Although commonly used to describe any custom item, bespoke is traditionally associated with tailoring.

Black Tie
Black tie is a dress code for formal evening events and is worn to many types of social functions. For a man, the major component is a dinner jacket or tuxedo, which is usually black but is sometimes seen in white.

Boutonniere

A boutonnière is a floral decoration worn by men, typically a single flower or bud. The word comes from the French boutonnière or buttonhole, which is the British term. The flower itself is often a carnation, which is most often white, while red remains a classic alternative.

Cashmere

An extremely soft and lightweight luxury fiber combed from the undercoat of the long-haired Kashmir goat. Cashmere has a soft and silky finish and is most commonly woven or knit to produce sweaters, suits, coats, and other winter accessories.

Chino

A type of cotton twill that can be finished with a smooth or mercerized brushed surface. Originally used as summer uniforms for the U.S. Army because of their durability.

Collar Stays

Collar stays are smooth, rigid strips of metal (such as brass, stainless steel, or sterling silver) rounded at one end and pointed at the other, inserted into specially made pockets on the underside of a shirt collar to stabilize the collar's points.

Corduroy

A fabric composed of twisted fibers that lie in distinctive vertical or horizontal rows. Each row, known as a wale, can vary in width. Corduroy wears well, has a soft luster, and is typically used for pants, sport coats, and shirts.

Cotton

Gathered from the seed pods of the cotton plant, this fiber is most often spun into yarn or thread and used to make a soft, breathable textile. Cotton is the most widely used natural-fiber cloth in clothing today; cotton fibers have a high degree of strength, durability, and absorbency. Egyptian cotton is considered to be the finest, with Sea Island as its domestic counterpart. Although less expensive, Pima cotton is also of high quality due to its extra-long staple fibers.

Crew Neck

A crew neck is a type of shirt or sweater that has a round neckline and no collar, often worn with other layers. The t-shirt crew neck was developed in 1932 as an undergarment that would absorb sweat and prevent shoulder pads of American football players from causing chafing. The United States Navy was the first of the United States armed forces to adopt the crew neck t-shirt.

Flannel

A soft woven fabric. Usually a twill weave that is slightly napped, or brushed on both sides for additional warmth and comfort.

Herringbone

A variation on a twill weave fabric, in which the twill is reversed, or broken at regular intervals, producing a distinctive V pattern resembling the skeleton of a herring fish.

Intarsia

A knitting technique used to create patterns with multiple colors. As with the woodworking technique of the same name, fields of different colors and materials appear to be inlaid in one another, but are in fact all separate pieces fit together like a jigsaw puzzle.

Jacquard

A fabric with a design woven into it. The word jacquard comes from Joseph Marie Jacquard, a nineteenth-century French inventor who created the special loom this elaborate fabric is woven on. The special loom attachment allows for any pattern, no matter how large, small or intricate to be woven in a fabric.

Merino Wool

A better quality wool yarn made from the fleece of merino sheep. Merino sheep are said to have the finest and softest wool of any sheep.

Oxford

A weave in which the warp (horizontal) has two fine yarns paired together and one heavier softly-spun weft (vertical) yarn, which gives the fabric a subtle basket weave look and a lustrous finish. Well known for men's shirts, it is also used for summer jackets and sportswear. Originated by a Scottish mill, oxford was one of four shirt fabrics named after famous universities, along with Harvard, Yale and Cambridge.

Paisley

A swirled tear-drop shape pattern commonly found in neckties.

Pique

A durable woven or knit fabric that is characterized by an allover textured pattern of raised parallel cords or fine ribbing. The most popular patterns are Birdseye, diamond, waffle and honeycomb.

Placket

A placket is an opening in the upper part of trousers or skirts, or at the neck or sleeve of a garment. Plackets are almost always used to allow clothing to be put on or removed easily, but are sometimes used purely as a design element.

Plaid

A fabric with a pattern of bars and stripes that cross each other at right angles. Plaid fabrics may be printed or woven and come in a variety of colors.

Split Yoke

This is the dress-shirt yoke. A one-piece yoke refers to a yoke that is constructed from a single piece of fabric, while a split yoke refers to a yoke which is split in the middle. The split is of course sewn together and you can see that the two pieces are arranged at an angle of one another.

Suit

A set of outer clothes made of the same fabric and designed to be worn together, typically consisting of a jacket and trousers.

Super Wools

Super wools are super-lightweight, high-twist wools pioneered by Italian mills. These fabrics are made using high-tech machines that spin wool lighter and finer than it's ever been spun before. The various grades of cloth are referred to as Super 100s, Super 120s, and Super 150s and so on, up to Super 200s.

Tasmanian Wool

A merino-quality type of wool that comes exclusively from the island of Tasmania, off the coast of Australia. The wool is taken only off the shoulders of the sheep, which produces the finest yarns. This quality of wool is used strictly for super 90's, super 100's and super 120's.

Twill

Fabrics created by interlacing the warp and weft so that the fabric has a diagonal slant or twill line. Twill fabrics have a front and a back side, unlike plain weave, where the two sides are the same. The face side of a twill fabric is the side with the most pronounced wale and is usually more durable, more attractive, and used as the fashion side of the fabric.

Conclusion

The *ultimate gentleman* is defined as a man who not only has a refined appearance and charismatic personality, but a man who is well-mannered and educated with high standards of proper behavior. The *ultimate gentleman* performs at the highest level in his role as a provider, leader, teacher, and relationship builder. These roles require a man to possess a strong character, to represent masculinity and manliness and to treat others with respect and courtesy.

My hope is that this handbook will not only influence men to be their best, but serve as a guide for those who have limited opportunities to view and learn from them. This small handbook can also be a valuable resource to help boys and young men from all backgrounds to become adult men who are positive and influential in relationships, family, church and community. I sincerely hope you or someone you know will find *The Ultimate Gentleman: The Handbook 2.0* a useful tool for personal growth and success.

Visit **www.UltimateGents.com** to explore our digital toolkit and blog dedicated to sharing tips and resources on how to become a gentleman of character, class and style.